ACKNOV

For my education a[...] ay I
particularly thank th[...] vati
Monastery at Great [...] ire,
England.

The literature and inspiration obtained there, all freely given, together with the stimulating environment of the monastery, have been essential in shaping my life for the better. The monastery can be found on www.amaravati.org

For my progress as a Life Coach I thank my clients. Without them I could never have properly appreciated the true scope of human potential. Without their courage in changing the way they think and behave, we could never have worked together to improve their lives. I can only hope that I have helped them as much as they have helped me.

For the design of this book I am indebted to my friend Howard Wright, without whose creative writing, publishing and IT skills and selfless assistance I would still be struggling to present my writing as something readable.

THE BUDDHIST LIFE COACH

A BRIEF GUIDE TO FREEDOM

NORMAN WHITWOOD

FOR JENNI, SOPHIE AND JEAN. MAY THEY FIND FREEDOM AND PEACE.

LCC Publishing
2 Parkinson Close
Wheathampstead
Herts AL4 8DP
Tel: +44 (0) 1582 833360

Web: www.lifeandcareerscoaching.com

First published 2012 © Norman Whitwood
The right of Norman Whitwood to be identified as the author
of this work has been asserted by him in accordance with the
Copyright, Designs and Patents Act of 1998.

ISBN 978-0-9563617-6-9

A catalogue record for this publication is registered with the
British Library.

2

www.lifeandcareerscoaching.com

INTRODUCTION

This book is intended to be a little different from typical writings on both Buddhism and Life Coaching. It is very much a basic introduction to both subjects, intended for anyone who believes, however tentatively, that they can be better and happier. Not only that, but that they deserve to be better and happier.

This book, though shorter than most, is nevertheless a labour of love. It is about love; for ourselves, for others and for life. After a long career running my own management Consultancy business, I turned to Buddhism and then Coaching following the death from cancer of my wife in 2001. Like millions of others in similar situations I learned the skills and patience required to carry on with earning a living, raise a young family alone and still remain positive and whole.

From that experience has grown an unshakable faith in my own potential, and in the potential possessed by everyone, whether or not it is understood or manifested. I have come to realise that the basic principles of Buddhism and Life Coaching offer tremendous hope to all who would endure and who would improve their lives. Not only hope, but also a clear, straightforward and practical path to the confidence and freedom which we all seek.

I love Buddhism and Life Coaching and the benefits that both practices can achieve. I have attempted to convey that love in this little book in the hope that it will strengthen others in their resolve to take control of their lives and make the very most of themselves, while they have the chance.

Becoming all that you can be will take time, perhaps a lifetime, but it is worth the effort. May this book help you to make a start.

Norman Whitwood   January 2012

*THEY DO NOT DWELL ON THE PAST
NOR BROOD ON THE FUTURE.
THEY ABIDE IN THE PRESENT,
THEREFORE THEY ARE RADIANT.*

THE BUDDHA

WHAT THIS BOOK IS ABOUT

Buddhism began 2500 years ago in northeast India. Life Coaching began in the 1970s in the USA. Despite the differences in time and impact they have much in common. This book is about linking the two in a way which you can easily follow and begin to make the most of your life.

They go together because they both address the basic, unchanging nature of human thought and behaviour. They are both founded, with natural logic, on human intelligence, learning and application. Both demonstrate in a very practical way how to understand ourselves and as a result, how to utilise the unknown potential possessed by every one of us.

We cannot change our lives without changing the way we think. This is universal law and this book explains how to begin to do both.

THE BUDDHA

The Buddha, whose real name was Siddhattha Gotama, was of high birth, living in luxury with his wife and family. Despite his own security and wealth he wanted to understand why there was so much unhappiness and pain all around. Like many of us today, he wanted to understand the cycle of human life and death: where we come from, why we are here and where we are going?

In order to find out he left everything behind and wandered homeless and penniless for six years, studying with the established traditional teachers of the time and enduring demanding practices in his search for the truth. He remained unconvinced and went his own way, eventually finding his own answers. When he did, he began teaching a new, practical philosophy and continued for 45 years, founding what we now call Buddhism, the fastest growing belief in the history of mankind and followed by millions of people. Buddha means The Enlightened One – the one who knows.

Life Coaching

Life Coaching grew out of psychotherapy and the need for a simpler form of treatment. Therapy was, and still is required by those who are suffering mental disturbance or trauma, but many patients were only confused or uncertain, not ill. As a result Life Coaching emerged as more direct and positive path to clearer thinking and decisive action. It was also quicker and less expensive in achieving tangible results. Coaching spread quickly and many thousands have trained as life coaches, but it has yet to be widely acknowledged as the powerful, healing and enabling process that it is. The result is that only a minority have experienced Coaching and realised their natural potential for living a fulfilled life.

Few Life Coaches are Buddhists but many Buddhists would make brilliant Coaches! For a Buddhist, our very humanity is explained simply and our path to maximum fulfilment made clear. For a Coach, our Values and our true needs and desires are made so clear that they are irresistible. For both, it is obvious what has to be done; for both it is clear that there is a path from delusion and confusion to a happy and meaningful life.

An enormous amount of material is available on both subjects but the basic principles of Buddhism and Life Coaching are straightforward and can be self taught. Ultimately they are *only* self taught! They are not just concepts. They are above all *direct experiences*. They have the capacity to affect us personally and deeply and from them we will develop self awareness and wisdom. They share one great eternal aspiration: to help us unconditionally to understand and realise our true potential for goodness and happiness and to live up to it.

This deliberately uncomplicated book explains the basic principles and how to begin our journey. It describes a clear and self-sufficient path to a happy and productive life. There is nothing here which has not been expounded in great detail nor been thoroughly and repeatedly proven in practice. What is different is the alliance of two incredibly positive and life changing practices, one ancient and one modern, with each deriving fresh power and relevance from the other.

May all who read it enjoy this brief guide to the gateway marked Freedom and on the other side, may they find what they seek.

THE MEANING OF LIFE

Millions have attempted a definition, including our cave-dwelling ancestors, Jesus Christ and Monty Python. Many of us have our own. But to Buddhists and Life Coaches the meaning of life lies in what we personally make of it. We may have a faith which sustains and guides us but, like all other creatures on Earth, we are born and we die and life is essentially what happens to us in between. What we call Life is only given purpose and meaning by the way we respond to it and how we live it.

Evolution, commerce and communication have bound all life on Earth together. That has resulted in interdependence, which we must acknowledge and develop if we are to enjoy a viable global future. As a result of our interdependence we are required to react in our lives to others and to our circumstances. But that does not in itself result in meaning.

Reaction and resignation to the events of our lives are not the same as proactive maximising of our potential. Making the effort to make the most of our lives is the path to meaning. Life is a like a long and interesting journey; the challenge, learning and enjoyment is in the travelling, not the arriving. There is actually no need to arrive at all. We are already 'there'. Everything we will ever need is already here, inside us, waiting for release. We are literally born ready.

It is how we respond to what we see and learn and how we think about what happens to us and the people we meet which gives it all purpose. But it is up to us individually to discover our potential on the way and make the most of our time. Life can ultimately be wonderful, liberating and full of joy, but we have to make it so.

Finding real meaning and fulfilment in your life is simpler than we might think, but it is not easy.

Nothing worthwhile ever is. Effort is involved!

BUDDHIST COACHING

The Buddha was just a man, not a god nor a prophet, and there is no supreme being, God or everlasting soul in his teaching. To a Buddhist we are what we are. We are what we see when we look in the mirror, no more and no less: flesh and blood, senses, perceptions, thoughts and consciousness.

These are the Buddhist Five Aggregates, which with

Energy make up the being which we call Me. The Buddha believed in the power of human capability, effort and intelligence. Also, in our innate ability to free ourselves from self-deception and the resulting unhappiness.

Life Coaching believes in and encourages exactly the same ideals and goals. Coaches are most definitely not gods or prophets but they also believe that what we see is very much what we get. The same components as everyone else, but with our own unique design and potential. Whatever our faith or belief, we will only attain true freedom by looking at our life, deciding to live it in the most fulfilling way and by doing something about it!

To live a life of meaning, the common factor between Buddhism and Coaching is the recognition of Reality, or seeing things as they are. Because we are made up of ever changing and interacting elements, uncertainty and potential disappointment are built into our lives. All our experience tells us this must be so. Both Buddhism and Coaching require us to acknowledge this and to be realistic about ourselves, about our lives and how we wish to live them. This may sound difficult, but fear not - there is a positive and well signposted Path to follow: The Four Noble Truths.

THE FOUR NOBLE TRUTHS

The Four Noble Truths, which were discovered and taught by the Buddha, constitute the very core of Buddhism, and in different terminology, of Life Coaching. What the Buddha worked out so long ago and what we all now acknowledge, is that life can often be difficult and a bit of a pain. For many, the pain can be real, lifelong and unremitting. For others there is violence, poverty, bereavement and loss. This is literal and often terrible pain, of which there is so much, too much, in the world.

What the Buddha meant however is the every-day dissatisfaction caused by ambition, disappointment and anger, is experienced by all of us. Life, with its highs as well as lows, is so impermanent isn't it? Nothing seems to last, even the good things.

The Buddha realised that this is what irritates and limlts us. He called it Suffering and even in the midst of safety and plenty we are often still unsettled. We still suffer! Buddhism and Coaching each lay the responsibility for that squarely with ourselves, but also teach that the solution too is very much in our own hands. Both provide a definition of our Suffering, but also a path and a strategy out of our uncertainty and doubt.

Within the Four Noble Truths lies the means to fully understand and to follow the Buddhist path – a path of calm self awareness and patience. Life Coaching provides a modern, practical and motivational vehicle for achieving the same goals, of self awareness, understanding, compassion, true confidence and wisdom.

Noble means of the highest moral order and importance.

THE FIRST NOBLE TRUTH

There is suffering. Everyone suffers, from the highest to the lowest and from the richest to poorest. This is something which we all share as part of our human existence. We suffer because there is desire, craving, fear, disappointment, ignorance, dissatisfaction, anger, doubt, discontent, confusion, loss and so on.

All these affect us at different levels of intensity and in different ways, but they are never far away for the simple reason that we largely create them ourselves. If we think about it, they all stem from our own personalities, perceptions and conditioning. This mental suffering is rarely caused directly by

particular events or relationships o
to us. It is the result of the mistaken
we *think* about them and these event
effects on our lives.

Unpleasant things and feelings do happen t
but it is not those things which actually cause
to suffer – it is the way we worry about them and
attach to them. If we can just view them in a more
dispassionate and detached way they would not be
such a problem. They might still exist, and require
urgent action, but they will do so separately from
us and in correct perspective. When seen like this,
the bad things become more controllable and the
good things even more enjoyable.

Suffering arises when we don't understand
ourselves and as a result create unnecessary
reactions to what is happening to us. If we see and
acknowledge these things and feelings for what
they really are, mostly as passing before us without
any reality or permanence, then we can both enjoy
or reject them with simplicity and calmness. It just
takes a little practice!

ring. It is our craving, to
If you think about it, the
ing becomes obvious. It
mple does not actually
it! Our ambitions and
against us when they do not
ruition, or when good times come to an end, which happens quite regularly! They fuel our discontent and frustration. This is not just about the things which we want, but also the things which we would like to be rid of, like stress and the fear of failure.

We would all like to be happy, fulfilled, successful and appreciated, but so often we fall short of our dreams. For many of us life just keeps coming up hollow and incomplete.

The Buddha taught that all this discontent is the result of our own attachment and entanglement in expectation and desire. Not desire in the sexual sense, but the craving for things, for achievement, recognition, peace, security and so on. We never stop wanting something, do we? Or wanting to be rid of something.

He worked out that if we just relaxed and got on with what is right for us, concentrating on what is in front of us, now, everything we need will arise and manifest itself. *This* is the universal law of attraction. In the same way the things and thoughts which we do not need and which are harming us, will cease and fade away; if you like, the universal law of natural rejection! If that all sounds a little optimistic, be assured that millions of people over the last 2500 years and in the world today have found it to be true.

THE THIRD NOBLE TRUTH

There is an end to suffering. It is achieved by ceasing to crave, to have and not have; by ceasing to grasp, at our emotions and the things we think we want. This is the way out of our discontent. It is in our own hands and it is very practical and totally attainable.

This is also the central truth and purpose of Life Coaching. This is the point at which established ancient wisdom and proven modern motivational technique really connect to offer a complete, inspirational and life changing opportunity.

THE FOURTH NOBLE TRUTH

There is a path out of suffering, which is to follow the Buddha's Noble Eight Fold Path. But before we move on, how do his teaching and revelations thus far relate to Life Coaching?

COACHING TRUTHS

Life Coaching is for ordinary people who have something blocking their progress. They come to Coaching because they face a frustrating situation which they cannot improve without external objective assistance. This is something which we all experience from time to time. The reason is that we cannot always see ourselves sufficiently clearly and objectively to think outside the box. We need to see it all with a fresh perspective and from a new viewpoint. We are suffering but we do not really know why or what to do about it. We are too close and too involved; in the Buddhist sense, too attached.

The result is that the problem never gets properly examined or sorted out. It goes on getting worse and the effects of that can be devastating. They can last a lifetime, all too often blocking us off from the innumerable opportunities to build a happy and fulfilled life which continually come our way.

Life Coaching helps by enabling us to take a fresh look at ourselves and our problem. It allows us to back off and rewind back to our basics - to detach from our problem - and see clearly, *probably for the first time*, what makes us tick. It supports and encourages us while we find out what we value in life and therefore what we truly want. It is a very short but momentous step from there to doing something about getting it!

When we are frustrated and unhappy we need to go back to our innermost needs because some of them at least are not being satisfied. It is as simple as that. Something deep down is at odds with what we are doing and unless we go there and check it out we will *never* know what it is. But going there is to venture into unfamiliar territory which is way outside our comfort zone. That is why we have a problem. Does that make sense?

Coaching like Buddhism guides us logically along the path into the unknown, with support and compassion and without judgement or criticism. The path is logical and very human. The consequence of which is a secure and caring environment in which to explore and develop our self awareness.

This is all a lot more fun than it may sound, as is Buddhism. Coaching and Buddhism are founded on basic human psychology and evolved, ingrained aspirations. We may not immediately understand why but the path will quickly become familiar, safe and enjoyable. We are not talking about therapy but about literally thinking our own way out of our dilemma, like finding our way out of a maze by staying calm and just learning and figuring it out.

We just need a little help and encouragement to move in this new direction and begin a new personal journey to self awareness, via the Coaching course or the Eight Fold Path, or both.

THE EIGHT FOLD PATH

Bear in mind that we are going back 2500 years and the terminology befits the time. The relevance of the Path however is as fresh and powerful as ever. It lies as it always has at the very heart of Buddhist belief and practical moral living. It has influenced and guided millions. So what is it?

The Path consists of eight steps or phases which cover the development of our self awareness and our subsequent moral actions. They are written in logical sequence and described in slightly varying terms, but once understood they will operate simultaneously as an holistic mind set. They are like the spokes of a wheel, all simultaneously supporting each other.

Buddhism, though non-theistic, is a very ethical belief system. It is based on the goals of impeccable unselfish thought and compassionate respectful behaviour towards all other beings. Accordingly the eight steps on The Path fall into the three major areas of honourable human aspiration, all of which make good human common sense: Wisdom, Ethics and Concentration. Right simply means living perfectly in accordance with virtue, wisdom and compassion, for yourself and for others. The terms vary but the meaning is always the same.

We will consider the Coaching parallels as we go through them.

- **Wisdom** is made up from Right Understanding and Right Intention
- **Ethics** from Right Speech, Right Action and Right Livelihood
- **Concentration** from Right Effort, Right Mindfulness and Right Meditation

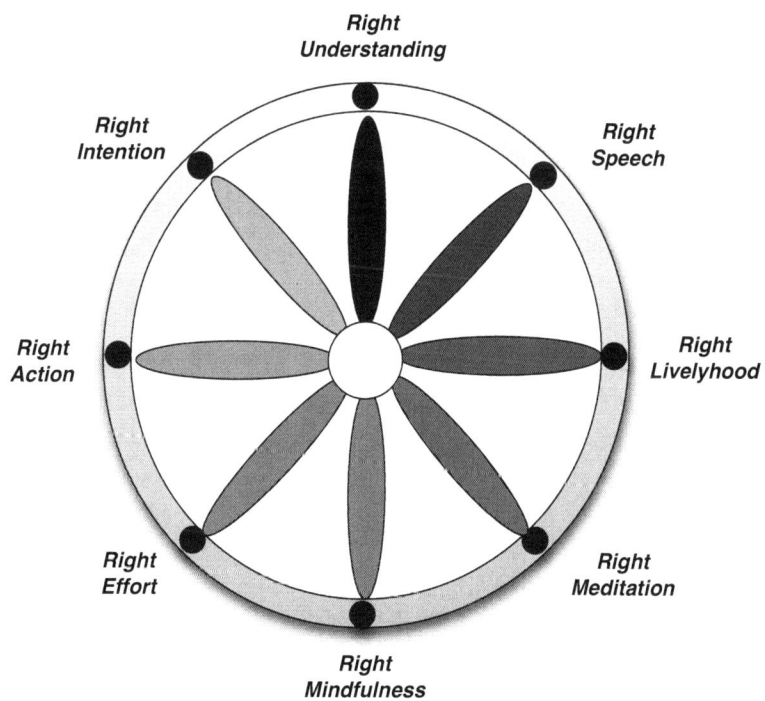

Wisdom

They say that Wisdom cannot be taught, it can only be learned. We learn Wisdom essentially from experience and reflection on our nature and human reality. It takes time and patience to acquire but like Virtue it becomes its own reward. You will know when you are wiser and feel better for it. So will everyone around you!

So how do we achieve this highly desirable state? Do we just wait for it to happen, or can we follow some sort of programme, or path, and make it a reality ourselves?

The answer is of course we can. Buddhism and Life Coaching are based on human common sense and compassion, internal reflection and action. We simply need to bring these into play in a positive and organised manner and to gently persist until the path becomes clear. So, how do we start?

RIGHT UNDERSTANDING.

We begin with Right Understanding, which comes from glimpsing our true nature and why we suffer.

If we consider the first three Noble Truths it is not difficult to see that they confirm what we have known for a long time: that we often lose contact with our calm and compassionate inner selves and instead exist largely at a superficial and materialistic level. And why wouldn't we? That is how, in the Western world especially, we are conditioned from birth by our environment and our expectations.

Life Coaching brings this self awareness to the surface by rewinding us back to our innermost Values. Coaching teases them out of the mists of our unconscious and into our consciousness, where we can consider and act upon them. Whether or not we are aware of it, our Values are what drive us. It is our Values which subconsciously form what we want and strive for in life. Before we can go much further then, we need to discover what they are and how far we are falling short of their fulfilment!

Thus Coaching and Buddhism are in accord at this crucial stage of our Path. Both involve looking inward and finding what is really driving us. They reveal our true Values and the discomfort caused by their absence in our lives.

Simply put, what Buddhists call Suffering is caused by clinging and attaching to our feelings. When we have the Right feelings, as a result of pursuing our true Values and our Path, we will exist in greater harmony with ourselves. *We will understand that this is the way things are, how they are meant to be and not how we imagine them to be.* This is the first step to letting go, relaxing and abiding in the here and now. It is the way to self knowledge, self awareness and true freedom.

RIGHT INTENTION

Now that we have begun to understand ourselves, what happens next? What do we actually do with this knowledge? We say that necessity is the mother of invention and this is a little like that. Once we begin to understand where we are losing out in our lives, we are literally faced with the necessity of doing something about it. It becomes an imperative because not to act negates a large part of our existence.

Consider for a moment. Having revealed exactly what we value and want most in life, and what is preventing our happiness, without any doubt, can we really stand by and do nothing about it? This is a one way door. Once we see clearly and pass through there is no going back.

Invention takes on the form of Intention. This is why we are suffering and this is what we need to find peace, so what are we going to do about it? What do we intend to do? We need a plan, but one which emerges naturally from our hearts; one which we can implement efficiently but with peace and patience, without clinging and frustration; one born of true awareness and which makes us happy. The more genuine and sincere the plan the less we will suffer. If we do lose our way, as we sometimes will, we will know where the path is and more easily return to it.

So what exactly are we to Intend? Essentially, Wisdom develops from direct experience, knowledge and reflection. In Buddhism these are born of selfless, loving humility and regular meditation. In Coaching, they are born of self awareness and logical analysis of our needs.

The common factor is the intention to take responsibility for ourselves, for what we think and what we do with our lives. This involves knowing ourselves and realising the need and right of others, as ourselves, to consideration and kindness. *Do for others what you have them do for you* is an ancient human aspiration which is as true for Buddhism and Coaching as any other human practice. It derives from basic innate humanity and the wise know instinctively how essential it is to our common welfare.

So, intend to be fully aware of ourselves and others; of their needs as well as our own; of their Suffering as well as our own; of their highs and lows arising and ceasing, coming and going; of our common need for time to learn.

Intend to improve our detachment and objectivity; our compassion for all living things; our understanding of our lives; our goals and objectives; our humanity.

Intend to know ourselves and what is really in our hearts and to share with others what is in theirs.

We are human and we will make mistakes. So when we do, intend to do a little better next time!

This gives rise to kamma, the good and not so good actions and consequences of every single thing we intentionally think, say and do. What we truly intend *will* come to pass. It is essential for a happy and guilt free life to do everything we can to intend good and avoid doing harm. Quietly being harm-less is as important as proactively being good and kind. These are supreme human qualities which will bring us everything we need in life. We just have to persist and wait.

ETHICS

Ethics are rules of conduct derived from moral principles. For many people these morals are derived from their religious faith and doctrinal teachings. For others with a secular and humanist view, Ethics follow naturally from common sense and the basic human compulsion to avoid harming others.

Buddhism and Life Coaching enable us to examine our motives for good, moral living in a practical, detailed manner. They provide a means to practice and learn from specific actions for promoting good and avoiding harm. Both provide a very clear framework within which ordinary people can discriminate between right and wrong, and speak and act accordingly.

RIGHT SPEECH

It goes without saying that, having got this far, we will care about what we say and how we say it. The first three Noble Truths of Buddhism and the Focus on Values exercise of Coaching will begin to reveal why we suffer. Either we are confused by clinging to our thoughts or we are living too far from our most important Values. When we are unhappy we are probably doing both. In fact, clinging to our thoughts instead of calmly considering and then letting them go - worrying in other words - is usually a direct result of being out of balance with our natural emotional needs.

Consider: if we are having problems it is likely that most others are too. It is from this realisation and that others may be worse off than us that human compassion arises. This is a cornerstone of Buddhism and Life Coaching also teaches us that we cannot have fulfilment at the cost of someone else's. If others are already unsure and confused, why would we make it worse with inappropriate or selfish speech?

As we develop our awareness, any careless or hurtful speech will increasingly hurt us too. We come to just know that it is wrong and we will suffer regret and guilt

Therefore abstain from all lying, backbiting and gossip. Do not be abusive, impolite, malicious or rude. Coaching would ask: what purpose does that serve? These things are empty and worthless and do only harm. Speak the truth or refrain from comment if that too is hurtful. Relax and speak appropriately and at the right time with helpful and useful comments. Be friendly and pleasant-why would you not be? Stop now and ask yourself: what purpose does it serve to be otherwise? It is very difficult to practice sometimes but awareness, kindness and restraint really are the only options which work in the long term.

RIGHT ACTION

The normal result of a Life Coaching Focus on Values exercise (more of this later) is an increased awareness of how much our Values, once revealed, mean to us. Also, a realisation of the consequences of following that awareness to a conclusion. The result is an increased sensitivity to cause and effect, as with exposure to the first three Noble Truths. Our actions are viewed in a different way, with avoidance of anything harmful becoming more important. Buddhists believe in the sanctity of all life and one of our key precepts is not to kill – anything. Also, not to steal or indulge in abusive drugs or confusing amounts of alcohol, to lead a moral life sexually and avoid deceit and help others to act in the same manner.

The message is clear: do nothing that will cause harm. Do only that which will do good. Both Coaching and Buddhism teach us to live in a focused manner by concentrating on worthwhile outcomes which improve ourselves and our environment.

In the same way we come to realise when something is simply the right thing to do. We will be pleased that we did it because it is a good thing which needed doing and not in a personal self congratulatory way. When we apply this attitude to our everyday activity things get done smoothly, calmly - now! Such is the power of non-attachment, objectivity and compassion for others.

RIGHT LIVELIHOOD

Life Coaching related to jobs and careers is particularly productive. By systematically revealing our Values we realise that we really do need to work to live, not the other way round! Also, that what we do for a living should reflect and include our most genuine aspirations. This is not easy to achieve. But so many of us are at odds with what we think we have to do to earn a living. We spend so much of our lives doing it that we have to try to get it right. Don't we?

Buddhism is equally practical about Livelihood. To begin with, if possible, avoid any work which involves killing or harm to others. Buddhists and many who come to Coaching expressly will not consider careers in the armaments, tobacco or alcohol industries, for example. They will not be involved in anything which will harm the environment and they often seek caring, social work or charity roles.

Buddhism and Coaching require us to carefully consider our jobs in the light of our Intention and our Values. These need to be clear and sincere. When we know beyond doubt that these come first, we can assess what we are doing against a reliable standard. Does it match up, or not? If not, what can we do about it? If we are well paid or enjoy the actual work, or it is difficult to change, is there a way to genuinely justify what we do?

Many of us are isolated from the final products or services which our organisation delivers. We are cogs in what are often huge machines. In such a situation we may not think much nor care about the end product. We might take comfort from performing our function with skill and efficiency, patience, goodwill and in reaping our just rewards. It may be very difficult to change, but we could ask ourselves if we could apply such transferable skills in another environment. If we are in business for ourselves, are we in the right industry and dealing with the right people to satisfy our Intention and Values?

In reality most organisational and business pursuits are beneficial or neutral. Doing the same thing but with a more enlightened mindset is usually the real challenge.

In the final analysis, both Buddhism and Life Coaching represent very personal journeys. The important issue therefore is how we conduct ourselves each day; how much we care about fulfilling our obligations, to ourselves and others. Also, how we treat our fellow creatures in our own sphere of influence - all of them! Even those we do not like or who cause us pain. So wherever we find ourselves, try to do good and avoid doing harm, for our benefit and that of the person next to us.

CONCENTRATION

Buddhist Concentration is about devoting our attention and focusing our efforts on everything we think and do. As with the other aspects of the Buddhist and Life Coaching path, there is a step by step process which we can learn and use at our own pace. There is no rush, but it is important to make a start and to begin to develop the habit of simply thinking about what we are saying and doing. This is preferably before we say and do it!

Our mind is a wonderful and essential facility, but we need to control it, our minds must not control us. This is the most important task if we are to change the way we think and, as a result, the way we live.

RIGHT EFFORT

No pain, no gain is the mantra for many self improvers. Discovering the best your heart and spirit can be and living up to it is no different. Effort is still required!

With Buddhism it is the effort and commitment to consider and reflect upon the elements of the Eight Fold Path and bring them into our everyday life. As with Coaching it is a gradual process, which should be persevered with but not rushed, absorbed but not forced. Each person will have their own speed and aptitude and it is important to build on solid foundations at every stage.

It is the effort required to think differently about ourselves and what we want. Will we keep on suffering from attachment to things and ideas, or will we try to clarify and simplify our thinking and take guidance? Will we commit and work our way through the Buddhist teaching or the Life Coaching programme for the sake of a better and happier future? Are we curious enough, or simply unhappy enough, to seek a new way?

Neither route is difficult and both relate directly to our basic nature and needs. Neither require long study nor academic skills. Both paths are clear but effort is required to set off and continue, one step at a time.

Without Right Effort nothing will change and we will miss the opportunity of a lifetime. It is that simple.

RIGHT MINDFULNESS

This is awareness of ourselves, of our bodies, thoughts and actions. One of the greatest pillars and gifts of Buddhism is the ability to 'abide in the present'. Dwelling on the past and brooding on the future - worrying again - is endemic and so stressful. We all do it don't we? Most of us find it difficult to be here, now, in the present, truly feeling the moment - this moment.

The self analysis and self knowledge which arises from Life Coaching leads to the same secure and calm self awareness; to the same confidence to relax and just be! The secret is to be *attentive*, all the time. Attentive to your feelings and those of the people around you; how the sun or the rain feels on your skin and how the breeze moves and smells; how the traffic and the birds sound; how our food tastes. The next time we eat why don't we really think about the different flavours involved?

Why don't we keep on chewing it to nothing and then pause and contemplate the experience before we take another mouthful? If that seems introspective and self conscious, be assured that it isn't!

It is simply relaxing and laying yourself open to whatever your senses are collecting and processing right now. The past is gone and the future isn't here yet. The only thing that is real is the present moment. Isn't it? Be here, be now! Be mindful of what is happening now.

We have all experienced that wonderful now-ness and clarity haven't we? After a long but satisfying day, or a difficult job successfully completed; on a beach watching the sunset; after a tough run or match. For many people, it is during prayer. Being 'in the zone' is effortless, contented and incredible, like being on a different mental plane altogether. With Right Effort and Right Mindfulness we can achieve that state as normal and, more important, still be fully awake and functional in the real world!

There is however one more essential factor. Yes, you have guessed it: Right Meditation

RIGHT MEDITATION

Meditation in its myriad forms has been a human activity since we started to feel and think. There are innumerable guides to and versions of what is actually one of the simplest, most natural and powerful experiences in human existence.

It naturally takes many forms but the result is always the same: getting in touch with ourselves. Meditation is simply a relaxation of our minds and bodies; a letting go. It is very much a normal human activity. We just need to channel that innate ability and focus on specifics to enjoy the full benefits.

What specifics do we need to focus on? For those of us who wish to examine and eliminate our suffering, the role of meditation is to direct our awareness towards our basic elements so that we can know them better. What that means is quietly considering our physical bodies, our feelings and emotions, our thoughts and the various events, large and small, which make up our lives.

As we consider these elements of flesh and blood, senses, perceptions, thoughts and consciousness, and energy, we become increasingly aware of them. Through them, we come to feel and know 'ourselves', the collective entity we call Me. We realise that our bodies, mental processes and experiences are what actually make up our existence. It is not a complicated idea!

The intention is not to become introverted or self conscious. It is to become truly aware of what and who we are; to know that we are an independent, functional and powerful beings who stand calmly alone and without fear. In time, beings with quiet and assured authority over every thought and action; beings which abides naturally in the present and see everything just as it is.

WHY MEDITATE?

There is no need to discuss here the many meditation and visualisation methods which abound. These can all be explored in due course. The simplest and arguably most effective way for beginners is Buddhist Insight Meditation. This was designed by the Buddha to bring practicality to centuries old transcendental and spiritual practices.

The Buddha was very pragmatic. He realised that although spiritual meditation was enlightening and empowering, something more directly related to the real human condition was also required. The same can be said for Life coaching. Self awareness and the clarity of purpose derived from Coaching are wonderful, but at some point we have to relate them to our everyday selves and our daily existence. Buddhism and Coaching have to make a difference here and now, in this life, in ways that create lasting change in us.

HOW IS IT DONE?

The purpose of meditation is simply to meditate. We are not trying to acquire or achieve anything. There is no need and no point in forcing the process or trying too hard. Simply do it, regularly and without preconceived objectives. The benefits will quickly become obvious and will accrue naturally, without undue effort. Meditation is a habit for life. There is no rush.

We need to be comfortable. Meditation can be done lying, sitting, standing and walking, at any convenient time. In the beginning, peace and quiet are required. First thing in the morning is popular, before embarking on the day's activities. This serves to prepare us well for the potential stresses before us. Last thing at night is also very productive. This allows us to reflect on and shed the cares of the day and to encourage a good night's sleep. This may be when we are lying in bed, but at other times the most popular position is sitting.

We can use the lotus position used by the Buddha and many others who possess the necessary flexibility, but this may require a little practice!

It is very important to notice our breathing. This is the time honoured method of stilling our minds and when our attention wanders, of quietly bringing it back to our meditation. The simple reason is that our breathing never ceases. Noticing the breath going in and going out, though our noses if that is our normal way, focuses us on something totally natural and relaxing.

Assuming that sitting is our choice, we first sit upright, on the edge of the bed or a chair. Keeping our back straight and head up, we place our hands on our knees or rest them lightly in our lap. Most people close their eyes to minimise distractions.

We then relax, maintaining only enough tension to keep our back and neck upright. We notice our breathing automatically going in and out, in and out. We then slowly scan our body from head to toe, sensing and releasing any tension that we feel. As we go we consider each part, paying particular attention to dropping and relaxing our shoulders. Taking our time we become aware of our entire body: is there tension, pain or stiffness? Concentrating on whatever we feel, we consider and reflect on the cause. We relax as much as possible and then move on, letting go of each sensation as we proceed. Satisfying ourselves that we are content at each stage, then letting go and moving on, is important. We become particularly aware of relaxing and letting go.

When we are relaxed and tranquil we consider our Feelings and Emotions. What are they at this moment? How have they arisen? Buddhism and common sense teach us that everything that arises also ceases. This is especially true of our Feelings and Emotions. The essential trick is to allow them to cease by considering them objectively and then simply letting them go. *Remember not to clutch them!*

Next come our Thoughts. Meditation is not about striving for an empty mind. It is about allowing thoughts to come, considering even the most worrying of them calmly and then letting them go. They are just thoughts. They are merely products of our own minds and our imagination and not real. They are the greatest cause of Suffering and we will learn to detach ourselves from them. *Let them go!*

The final step in our Insight meditation is to consider Events, or our most recent experiences and happenings. Like our Body, our Feelings and Emotions and our Thoughts, we need to bring them into our consciousness without fear. We then need to consider them for what they are, perhaps decide what we are going to do about them, or to put them aside for another time, *then let them go!*

WHAT DOES IT ACHIEVE?

By systematically considering these main elements of our existence we will rationalise and order what can be a chaotic, unmanageable jumble. Just considering each piece of our personal jigsaw in isolation will bring them into correct perspective. We will see them as they really are, that is largely insignificant and easily managed. We can then allow them to fade away.

The result is a clear and relaxed mind with nothing left to think about. This is important. We are not trying to achieve or acquire anything new. We are simply de-cluttering and discarding what we do not need. At this point we allow ourselves to simply be, here and now, in the company of no-one but ourselves. We are in touch with our permanent and irreducible core, which is always there regardless of the stress and confusion of our conscious world.

Thinking is overrated. Don't be afraid to switch it off!

As we gain self knowledge we attach less and less to the things which formerly concerned and worried us.

We still experience happiness and sadness, but we gain the insight to see these as arising and ceasing: we gain the confidence to let them come and go. We realise how substantial and independent we are and that we don't need to hold on to them. As a result we let them go once they are done. Eventually we will cease to suffer from them and begin to just be.

We come to know that feelings are not us. They are mind products and temporary, whereas the inner calm and assurance which grow in us are eternal.

It is very simple and natural. The more often we visit this quiet and impregnable place inside us the greater the strength and confidence we will derive from being there. There will come a time when this calm, unconscious awareness of ourselves, now, will become our default state. We may not quite know how we got there and it will take time, but with persistence we will arrive in the calm and everlasting present.

Loving Kindness

No writing about Buddhism or Coaching, no matter how brief, would be complete without discussing Loving Kindness.

Extending loving kindness to all creatures lies at the very heart of Buddhism. If we think about it, all but the most callous individuals will at some time be affected by love or kindness towards others. It sometimes requires a particularly moving or tragic experience but they will arise in most of us sooner or later.

So feelings of loving kindness and empathy are normal human emotions. Our problem is that we are often too busy or too preoccupied with ourselves to allow them to arise.

Buddhism brings them back to centre stage, as specific intentions. Life Coaching provides a similar, practical beginning by restoring our self awareness and our in-born aspiration to kindness and respect. It is then only a short step to considering the rights of all others to the same things, isn't it? If we are entitled to these things, isn't everyone else?

If we suffer then others must suffer too. Do we

really want to increase their suffering, or can we treat them in a way which relieves it and which helps and supports them? With self awareness comes genuine self confidence. With self confidence comes greater patience and compassion for the world and everything in it.

Loving kindness is the wish for happiness for all beings, including ourselves. It transcends personal love and the highs and lows which go with it. It seeks no acknowledgement, nor any reward.

The Buddhist path deliberately and inevitably develops our mind towards it; Life Coaching provides the self knowledge and unshakable confidence to care openly and without fear for all those around.

What happens next?

Well, we have to *do* something! With both Life Coaching and Buddhism the aim is to get from where we are as people to where we would like to be - to where we *should* be. In order to achieve this fundamental and life changing shift, we have to work on some basic issues.

To begin, we have to identify where we really wish to be in clear personal terms. We have to find out how we *really* want to live.

Then, we have to identify how we are living now and admit that, for whatever reasons, it simply may not match up to where we should be. There is something missing and we need to see what it is.

We begin by identifying what we should be doing and what we are actually doing. Then we can honestly admit that these are the true realities - this is how our life really is. Because there is no escaping this truth we are motivated to examine the differences between the present situation and our new intentions. We can then work in practical ways to bridge the gap between them.

Ok, so where do we want to be? What do we want?

We think we know, don't we? Health, happiness, security, love, money, house, decent car, holidays... But how many of us have thought this through and really worked it out? It is not easy is it? In our heart of hearts what do we want? Exactly *how* are we going to be happier?

One sure way to find out is to consider what we Value, what we believe in and why they are the most important issues for us. If we can establish what they are we will see more clearly what is missing in our lives. In other words, what we most want.

FOCUS ON VALUES

Consider the Focus on Values exercise at the back of the book. This is a common Life Coaching tool and this particular list of Values is evolving, with the help of clients, from years of Coaching practice.

We use the list by carefully considering which Values are important to us. Each will mean different things to different people. That is the point. The purpose is to find out what really means most, to us, *individually*. We need to know, deeply and without doubt, what we care about. Then as a result, we can begin to understand ourselves and what we want.

There is no hurry and we can make as many attempts as we wish. If there are Values which we would like to add, or perhaps change to better reflect our individual perception, then we can do so. We carefully consider which Values *mean* something to each of us. It need be no more complicated than that. If a word means nothing then move on. Which of them would you like in your life, whether you have them now or not?

Most people find this challenging and one way is to work in reverse by eliminating those which have no or little meaning. This will eventually leave those which do. Take your time and think about it. This is the beginning of Right Understanding, of self awareness and of how we fit into the world. This is important!

Once we have our Values identified, our present existence is brought into focus. The shortfall compared to our ideal becomes clear. Buddhist belief relates to a range of eternal human ethics and aspirations. Although our Coaching Values may be more specific to our own history and circumstances, there will be a clear connection between them and core Buddhist standards.

When and *only* when we have selected our most important Values, we can list them in priority order. The difference between some may be marginal, but we need to persist. This is fundamentally important because the resulting list will reveal our deepest life wishes and how we would like to relate to our present situation and to the world around us. Also, this revelation will establish our Life Intent, the essential driving force in our lives. We need to get it right. If this is what we really want, need and deserve, we have to go and get it!

Next, we check out our Values, beginning at the

top of our list and working our way down. Now, one at a time, we consider how we measure up to our own aspirations? How much of each Value do we have now and how much are we falling short in our lives, our jobs, or our relationships? For each Value, what is the difference between what we want and what we actually have? For some Values we will be content that we have what we need, but for others there will be an uncomfortable or painful void. How much do we feel and regret our missing fulfilment?

Go back to Buddhist **Right Intention**. Through our Values we have become more self aware and as this understanding develops there is no resisting the certainty of what we must do. To do nothing means a lot of wasted time and wasted life - our life.

So, first we Intend to take responsibility for ourselves and what is going to happen to us. What we truly intend *will* happen. Make it so!

Now would be a good time to have a conversation with a Life Coach, or a Buddhist, or both. If possible, with a Buddhist Coach! Together we would examine those Values which we want most, but which occur least in our life. What are we doing and who are we doing it with which prevents them from arising?

What are we not doing and who are we not doing it with? What behaviour, by us or others around us, is stopping from living up to our most precious ideals? Think! This is Right Understanding, right here, right now! Write down everything in our life which is blocking the way forward.

FOCUS ON DAILY LIFE

Now look at the Focus on Daily Life exercise. This is another commonly used Coaching tool which is practical and powerful. This also is a guide and once we are familiar with the concept we can add, separate or change the life aspects to suit our individual thoughts.

Taking our time and thinking it through, with our top Values in mind, we mark ourselves for each aspect of our daily life. Where we score 5 or 6 we can be satisfied. Which Values are in place and strong there? Wow! We have got something right! Where we score 4 or less we consider honestly what we can do to improve the score. Be honest. What have we been putting off or pretending is not a problem? This is the moment to check the reality of our life and take small, practical steps to make it better.

For example, where there is score of 2, what can we do to improve it to 4? Where there is a 4, what more can we do to reach 6? Are there any at 1? How much can *they* be improved? There is usually something that can be done so do not be put off by a very low score. How can we get a 1 to 2 or 3? Make a start!

Consider each aspect carefully. There is no hurry. *Exactly* what can we do or start to do – tomorrow. Write it down now.

This is not a theoretical or writing exercise. It is a *doing* exercise. But we do need to note the actions which we have agreed with ourselves and decide which we are going to do first. However, we do not decide to decide, or make excuses: we just do. It is simply a question of which is first. Hold that thought: it is very important. It may not be feasible to do all we would like, at first, but we do something - *now*.

Begin to get the action habit!

We can begin with the actions which will bring the most distant Values nearer to our lives. There may be practical difficulties in doing that, so we note those and consider how to overcome them later.

Right now, we move onto the next most important and achievable item. We find a starting point.

We are thinking now about our Values and our actions to achieve them. Whatever the obstacles, *start*! We use our Focus on Daily Life issues to see how our Values work in our everyday lives.

This is how **Right Intention** arises and translates into **Right Action**. We have now found that there are very important Values which are deficient in our lives. We can see from the Daily Life issues where they can be strengthened in practical ways. We will still need time to work on details and our understanding, but the path is clearer. We can see where to go and we therefore intend to begin the journey - right now.

In order to maintain that Intention we consider and implement our actions methodically. We do not forget any but we proceed one at a time, achieving and building self awareness and confidence as we go. We do not rush. This may take some time! The important thing is that it is happening and that we are focusing, learning and growing.

These simple but revealing exercises *will* start us on the path to Right Understanding, Right Intention and Right Action. The beginnings of Wisdom through self awareness will arise, with practical changes in our lives and our work following on at a natural pace.

This process of investigation will inevitably expose

what is wrong in our lives and in our jobs and careers. **Right Livelihood** is that which causes least conflict in our minds and hearts. However, we need to remember first that this conflict may not be the result of a wrong livelihood: it may be the result of our wrong attitude to it.

So, we need to examine first if we can change our thinking and actions in order to manifest our top Values in the same situation. Changing livelihoods is not that easy so first we need to be sure that we have made the best of what we have. This is a great opportunity to review our work life, but we have to honest and realistic.

We need to check the aspects of our Focus on Daily Life for guidance. Many will relate to our work and how we feel about it.

We will develop a new, clearer understanding of our whole situation. We can pinpoint where action is needed. If necessary, we can now carry out our own research or seek specialised guidance and support.

The more we focus, the more focused we become.

This becomes a powerful habit and we need to be

focusing on the right things. Once we know where we want to go we can seek help anywhere. We can be open and freely search for support wherever we can find it. Why shouldn't we? Those around us will admire and respond to our willingness to improve and grow. It is the rest of our lives which we are preparing for and it is truly important that we do our best. *So, ask for help! Seek advice!*

THE END OF THE BEGINNING

Changing the way we think so that we can change our lives takes courage. Admitting that we are not always right and that we do not have all the answers requires humanity and humility. We are often shaken out of our complacency by a traumatic experience or a shock. We are almost forced to change our attitudes sometimes because we simply cannot cope using the old thought mechanisms and methods. Sometimes, a new way *has* to be found.

But we do not have to wait to be forced into change. If we make the effort now, Buddhist and Life Coaching principles will always provide a solid, permanent foundation amidst the changing circumstances around us. Beginning now and developing them over a lifetime will ensure that they never let us down.

We should acknowledge also how much our self awareness and mindfulness will help and support others in their times of need. We become known for our calmness, patience and wisdom. We will give them freely without thought of reward.

The Buddhist Coaching way is one of compassion,

love and enthusiasm for life and for everything that lives, including ourselves. By pursuing our understanding through the Four Noble Truths, and our Values and Focus on Daily Life through the Eight Fold Path we will find our own true direction.

These together are the bedrock upon which we can build a lifetime's reflection and learning and reach our own personal fulfilment.

We will at times slip from our path but we will always know where it is and be able to return, in *light* and in darkness.

May this book inspire a new beginning. May all who read it be encouraged to abide in the present and find enlightenment and peace.

For further information visit:
http://www.lifeandcareerscoaching.com

EXERCISES

FOCUS ON VALUES

Carefully select the 12 most important to you, whether or not you have them in your life at the moment. Please add others if you wish.

Achievement	Family	Kindness	Security
Artistic	Friendship	Knowledge	Self Discipline
Assertiveness	Fun	Leadership	Self Esteem
Autonomy	Faith	Learning	Service/ Helping
Awareness	Flexibility	Listening	Selflessness
Beauty	Freedom	Love	Spirituality
Calmness	Growth	Optimism	Stability
Caring	Happiness	Patience	Standards
Challenge	Health & Vitality	Peace	Status
Confidence	Honesty	Physical Activity	Strength
Control	Humility	Power	Tolerance
Creativity	Humour	Pride	Tradition
Discovery	Individuality	Recognition	Truth
Empathy	Integrity	Respect	Understanding
Enjoyment	Intimacy	Responsibility	Variety
Excitement	Justice	Religion	Wisdom

FOCUS ON DAILY LIFE

Consider each of these aspects of your everyday life and rank them carefully from 1 - 6. A ranking of 1 means that you are very dissatisfied and 6 that you are very satisfied. Please add more or separate these if you wish.

Values & Beliefs	1	2	3	4	5	6
Personality	1	2	3	4	5	6
Direction & Goals	1	2	3	4	5	6
Education & Training	1	2	3	4	5	6
Self Confidence	1	2	3	4	5	6
Career & Business	1	2	3	4	5	6
Family & Home life	1	2	3	4	5	6
Stress	1	2	3	4	5	6
Personal Growth	1	2	3	4	5	6
Body Image & Appearance	1	2	3	4	5	6
Health & Fitness	1	2	3	4	5	6
Relationships & Friendships	1	2	3	4	5	6
Leisure activities	1	2	3	4	5	6
Social Life	1	2	3	4	5	6
Money	1	2	3	4	5	6

LCC Publishing ©2012

NORMAN WHITWOOD

After qualifying as a mechanical engineer, Norman Whitwood spent 35 years as a management consultant, running his own company and specialising in improving organisational efficiency.

Working in a variety of sectors and with a wide range of individuals led him to change management, mentoring, training and then to Life Coaching. He qualified as a coach and began to practice full time in 2005.

Both personal circumstances and his own deep interest in people and life's lessons and opportunities led him to Buddhism. Since 2002 he has followed a Buddhist path, simply, but with total conviction in the basic, common sense principles of that great, 2500 year old belief.

Communicating with, understanding and helping others has always been his driving force. What do they really want? How can he best work with them to achieve it? How can they best buy into the process and optimise their input? How will he and they know when the programme is finished and when they can be left to go on alone?

He has found that the answers to these and many other questions can be found along the Life Coaching and Buddhist paths.

Norman practices full time as Life and Careers coach in Wheathampstead in Hertfordshire, England and can be found on:

*Http://*www.lifeandcareerscoaching.com